2

Sally Congdon-Martin

Other Schiffer Books By The Author:
Emerging Fashion Designers 1. ISBN: 978-0-7643-3600-3. $39.99

Other Schiffer Books on Related Subjects:
Accessorizing the Bride: Vintage Wedding Finery through the Decades. Norma Shephard. ISBN: 0-7643-2185-4. $49.95
Dress Shirt Design. Malie Raef. ISBN: 978-0-7643-2723-0. $79.95
Fashion Plates: 1950-1970. Constance Korosec & Leslie Piña.
ISBN: 0-7643-0438-0. $39.95
Signature Prints: Jet-set Glamour of the '60s & '70s. Roseann Ettinger Clothing Modelled by Amber Lee Ettinger.
ISBN: 978-0-7643-2896-1. $39.95

Designed by John P. Cheek
Cover design by Bruce Waters
Type set in Felix Tilting/News Gothic BT

ISBN: 978-0-7643-3791-8
Printed in Hong Kong

Cover Model: Sally Lotter
Photographer: Claire Zeller Barclay
Hair & Makeup: Sarah Brown

Schiffer Books are available at special discounts for bulk purchases for sales promotions or premiums. Special editions, including personalized covers, corporate imprints, and excerpts can be created in large quantities for special needs. For more information contact the publisher:

Published by Schiffer Publishing Ltd.
4880 Lower Valley Road
Atglen, PA 19310
Phone: (610) 593-1777; Fax: (610) 593-2002
E-mail: Info@schifferbooks.com

For the largest selection of fine reference books on this and related subjects, please visit our website at **www.schifferbooks.com**
We are always looking for people to write books on new and related subjects. If you have an idea for a book please contact us at the above address.

This book may be purchased from the publisher.
Include $5.00 for shipping.
Please try your bookstore first.
You may write for a free catalog.

In Europe, Schiffer books are distributed by
Bushwood Books
6 Marksbury Ave.
Kew Gardens
Surrey TW9 4JF England
Phone: 44 (0) 20 8392 8585; Fax: 44 (0) 20 8392 9876
E-mail: info@bushwoodbooks.co.uk
Website: www.bushwoodbooks.co.uk

DEDICATION

This book is dedicated to my mother & father, Josh and Liddy—I couldn't design a better group of people to call my family.

ACKNOWLEDGMENTS

Gathering the many wonderful images in this book was no small task and it would not have been possible without the help and support of the contacts at the participating schools. Thanks to Edith Mead Barker at Academy of Art University, School of Fashion, Genevieve Dion at Drexel University, Marilyn Hefferen at Fashion Institute of Technology, Sondra Grace at Massachusetts College of Art and Design, Amanda Mott at Moore College of Art & Design, Clara Henry and Andrew Davis at Philadelphia University, Robin Mollicone at Pratt Institute, Catherine Andreozzi at Rhode Island School of Design, Stephanie Thomas at Savannah College of Art and Design, Elizabeth (Missy) Bye at the University of Minnesota, Dr. Gindy Neidermyer and Kathryn Kujawa at The University of Wisconsin-Stout, and Dr. Carol Salusso at Washington State University.

Thanks to the Council of Fashion Designers of America, particularly Amy Walbridge Ondocin, for their support in distributing the call for submissions.

Many thanks to the folks at Schiffer Publishing for their continued guidance through the book building process, and support of the project.

Thanks to all the photographers who contributed their images to the book (named throughout) and including David Gehosky for Drexel University and Eli Schmidt and Adam Kuehl for SCAD. Finally, thanks to the students who allowed their work to be shown in this book.

CONTENTS

INTRODUCTION

Fashion is the type of challenging industry where the experienced typically advise hopefuls entering the fray, "if there is *anything* else in the world you might like to do, you should do that instead." For most designers, I think, there is no choice. And without a degree in fashion, a career in fashion is extremely difficult to develop. Core curriculum for fashion design programs generally includes patternmaking, draping and sewing, textiles, design theory, fashion illustration, costume history, and covers everything from swimwear to sportswear to couture. The endeavor to learn all this while honing one's own creativity and point of view is notoriously intense, sleepless, and stressful. The pages of this book contain the labors of love of hopeful young designers for whom there is nothing in the world they would rather do.

The most enjoyable part of compiling this book is seeing young designers really "go for it," and make design decisions without the shadow of the marketplace bearing down; in other words they can be artists. That is not to say those featured in this book haven't made viable clothes—in fact even as students these designers clearly grasped the needs and/or aesthetics of their potential consumers. These pages show what happens when designers have autonomy to make their own design decisions rather than having it come from a boss or team, which is rare in the "real world." Fashion school is a time where students can be most daring, to take chances to find out what works. The result can be experimental, exuberant, and precocious but above all *personal*.

The intent of *Emerging Fashion Designers* is to showcase the work of these dedicated young designers, and bring together the products of fashion design programs across the United States. Included is work by more than 60 designers representing 12 schools.

As with the first edition, the process of selection began with the schools. I asked the programs to choose the designs and illustrations that best represent their programs, from designers who mostly graduated in 2010 and are entering the industry now. Then I sorted through those submissions, selecting designers based on various criteria, including originality in concepts, exceptional construction and illustrative skill, marketability, and in some cases all of the above. The work is organized alphabetically by designer, with inspirations and materials for their designs listed to give a well-rounded understanding of their work. Additionally, the designers are indexed by schools in order to give a snapshot of what different programs have to offer.

I had no trouble finding a diversity of perspectives from the students' work of 2010; in these pages you will find pieces that range from avant-garde to sporty, from children's wear to tailoring and everything in between. Some work will amaze you with its construction and engineering, like Christina Lord's immaculate collection of lingerie, and some work wows with its use of color, like Marina Popska's swirling, nature-inspired knitwear. Some work should be hanging in Barney's, like Brittany Oliver's tonal sportswear; some belongs in a museum like timothy k.'s silk cocoon gown. Some work is inspired by the thought provoking, like Hailey Desjardin's extremely wearable take on visual disorders, and some comes from a truly unexpected place, like Jessica Jung McCorkle's interpretation of the beauty of fly fishing. The common denominator across these pages may just be the skill and talent of the young designers, and the bright careers they have ahead of them.

Compounding the usual competitiveness in the fashion world, designers entering the industry now continue to face an economy that makes it increasingly difficult to find work with a degree in fashion. I hope this book brings recognition and opportunity to these students and appreciation for the schools that have shaped them.

The work in this book belongs to the designers, and I thank them for allowing it to be in print.

THE
DESIGNERS

CHRISTINA ARMSTRONG

UNIVERSITY OF MINNESOTA

Inspiration: Sparked by a winter trip to Death Valley, California, the designer was moved by the sun bleached pale December hues and the juxtaposition between cracked earth and lush flora.

Materials: Hand illustrated in pencil, outlined in Adobe Illustrator, and filled in Adobe Photoshop

Advised by: Chad Sowers

DIANA BADER
DREXEL UNIVERSITY

Inspiration: Exaggerated silhouettes, unique texture, and sleek form inspired the development of this collection. The designer incorporated leather, hair, and gleaming feathers to create an unusual variety of surfaces within her collection.

Materials: Leather, hair, feathers

Photograph courtesy of Drexel University

Photographs courtesy of Drexel University

CAROL BERGER

UNIVERSITY OF MINNESOTA

Inspiration: This garment was inspired by the softness of nature against the composition of modern architecture. The shibori dyed silk was inspired by Claude Monet's paintings of water lilies.
Materials: Silk, leather, hardware closure on back
Advised by: Elizabeth Bye

Photograph courtesy of Stephanie Hynes, www.stephaniehynes.com

EVAN BIRCH

RHODE ISLAND SCHOOL OF DESIGN

Inspiration: "Limiting myself to two colors, navy blue and black, throughout this experiment, I found how to balance and make fluid the collection and how each piece could relate to another piece in the collection. Through the use of machine knitting and the technical skills of tailoring, I have created a collection that is not only striking individually but strong as a whole."

Materials: Machine knit Spring wool, leather trim

Advised by: Catherine Andreozzi

Photograph courtesy of Claire Zeller Barclay; hair & make-up by Sarah Brown

Photographs courtesy of Claire Zeller Barclay; hair
& make-up by Sarah Brown

DANIELLE BLUM

FASHION INSTITUTE OF TECHNOLOGY

Inspiration: "I was inspired by vintage and modern cycling uniforms. I decided to use merino wool for the sweater and pant because the authentic vintage jerseys were constructed out of merino as well. The color story of the vest was inspired by an actual Cinelli brand cycling jersey."

Materials: 100% wool yarn, metal snaps

Materials: Markers and colored pencils

Photograph courtesy of Michelle Feffer

Photograph courtesy of Michelle Feffer

Photograph courtesy of Doug Congdon-Martin, Schiffer Publishing

LEAH C. BOSTON
MOORE COLLEGE OF ART AND DESIGN

Inspiration: The inspiration for this collection comes from the designer's travels to London, England, and her photographs of the Royal Guard as well as the city surroundings.
Materials: Wool, silk, leather, and chains
Advised by: Linda Wisner & Le Tran

Photographs courtesy of Jeff Cohn/FashionandAdvertising.com

Photographs courtesy of Jeff Cohn/FashionandAdvertising.com

RINAT BRODACH

ACADEMY OF ART UNIVERSITY, SCHOOL OF FASHION

Inspiration: An androgynous night out, with the hopes of Dorian Gray "to be young forever," is balanced with the style and mischief of Marchesa Luisa Casati, the fashionable heiress and muse to many artists. An additional inspiration is the thoughts and images of what people do in the dark in underground venues, in the bathrooms … and how clothes can be twisted, folded, caught on undergarments, then unknowingly worn into public view, accidentally looking intentional and stylish.

Materials: Wool, polyester, hand-dyed silk taffeta, "created" fabrics combining lace and latex (for shirt and short dress)

Advised by: Simon Ungless, Director of Fashion

Photographs courtesy of Randy Brooke

LUCY C. BUTLER
DREXEL UNIVERSITY

Inspiration: Geometric and organic shapes found in urban architecture inspired Lucy to design a collection of knitted sportswear. The grids formed by buildings, windows and city blocks became color-blocked expressions in her garments. She experimented with tubular and full-fashioned knitting and paired the knits with some wovens for balance.

Photographs courtesy of Drexel University

JESSICA CASTELLANO

RHODE ISLAND SCHOOL OF DESIGN

Inspiration: "My inspiration was drawn from the conflict of a career in music and a career in fashion. I grew up in a fairly isolated town in the Pocono Mountains of Pennsylvania, where combination cigarette-superstore and auto-repair centers outnumbered fashion outlets twenty-to-one. My goal in life was to be a classical pianist. My inspiration was from composers such as Beethoven and Bach...I wasn't exactly surrounded by the avant-garde, yet I always had fun using my creativity, my spot on the hand-me-down chain, and my pack rat tendencies to make outfits that made me look and feel good. This is when I realized that my passion was behind the sewing machine... Since this decision was such a milestone in my life, I wanted to incorporate it into my collection. I drew colors and dying techniques from the era of my once loved idols and I mixed it with the new techniques of my new idols in the fashion world. Burning and fraying the edges of these elegant tea/coffee hand-dyed and hand-pleated elegant fabrics show the conflict of my decision."

Materials: Silk chiffon, silk georgette, Italian silk, stretch tulle, nylon tulle, leather, silk and polyester lining, brass buckles and zipper

Advised by: Catherine Andreozzi

Photograph courtesy of Claire Zeller Barclay; hair & make-up by Sarah Brown

Photographs courtesy of Claire Zeller Barclay; hair & make-up by Sarah Brown

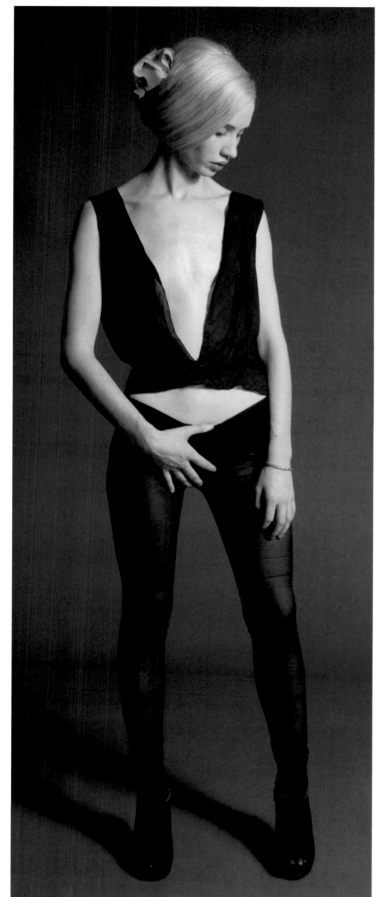

Photographs courtesy of Claire Zeller Barclay; hair & make-up by Sarah Brown

YUZUAN CHENG
Delphina Star Rodriguez, Textile Design

Inspiration: The "big suit" worn by David Byrne of The Talking Heads, David Bowie's *Ziggy Stardust* looks, and men's 1950s embroidered vintage shirts inspired this collection. The objective was to create a unisex collection, bridging men's wear and women's wear and incorporating traditional men's tailoring with hints of femininity. The color palette is vintage-inspired with color-blocks of peach, canary yellow, white, and pearl grey.

Materials: Pima cotton, cashmere wool, and organza
Textiles: Illustrated, hand-cut and laser-cut images, bonding, discharge and pigment screen-printing.
Advised by: Simon Ungless, Director of Fashion

Photographs courtesy of Randy Brooke

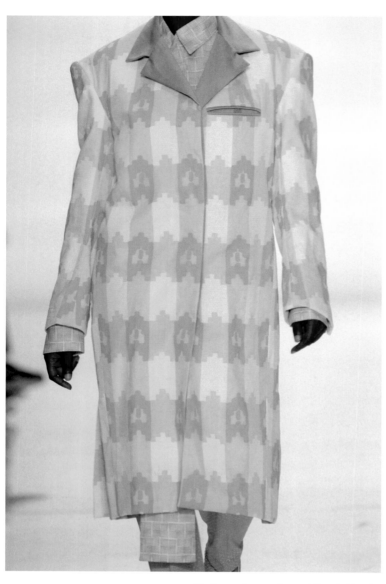

Photographs courtesy of Randy Brooke

ESTHER EUNJIN CHO
FASHION INSTITUTE OF TECHNOLOGY

Inspiration: "After traveling in Barcelona, I was mesmerized by Antonio Gaudi's architecture. I still remember sitting outside for a while just staring at the *Sagrada Familia* in awe on a sunny day. It was really hard to grasp everything in one sight. The patterns and shapes that are used in my garment were inspired from Gaudi's work. However, to lend my personal spirit, I used pastel tones of light blue and lavender to create a lovely look."

Materials: Kid mohair and cotton yarn

Advised by: Professor Michael Seiz

Photograph courtesy of Ho Chang

ABDO DAGHER
FASHION INSTITUTE OF TECHNOLOGY

Inspiration: Tropical flowers and their many layers inspired this design.
Materials: Pima cotton
Advised by: Rebeca Velez-San Andres

Photographs courtesy of Doug Congdon-Martin, Schiffer Publishing

Inspiration: Cottages often found in Canada inspired these designs.
Materials: Marker and colored pencil
Advised by: Steven Stipelman

Inspiration: Curtains and drapery inspired these designs.

Inspiration: These designs were inspired by the flowers petals and bright colors found in a Spring garden.

JULIA DAWSON
WASHINGTON STATE UNIVERSITY

Inspiration: This collection was inspired by an imagined futuristic, post-apocalyptic race of women who have survived and adapted to their environment with cockroach-like style and tenacity. The target market is modern women such as musicians or artists who are not afraid to wear innovative, daring outfits for special occasions.

Materials: Leather

Advised by: Dr. Yoo-Jin Kwon and Dr. Catherine Black

Photographs courtesy of Robert Hubner

Inspiration: In honor of the sustainability, this project was intended to demonstrate how being sustainable could result in intriguing design. We were to select a material to recycle; my choice was the very bags we collect from being fashionistas!
Materials: Department store paper bags
Advised by: Dr. Yoo-Jin Kwon and Dr. Catherine Black

BIANCA DEPIETRO

PHILADELPHIA UNIVERSITY

Inspiration: This fall evening wear collection was inspired partly by the play *No Exit* by Jean-Paul Sartre, where three characters with deeply sinful pasts meet in hell. "I was interested in the idea of what lies beneath the surface of a person. If you start to peel away all of their layers, darker traits, and secrets can be revealed... The three gowns I created are multi-layered, signifying the peeling away. Each gown is accented with distressed fabric, dye, hand crochet work, and beading."

Materials: Duchess satin, silk dupioni, silk shantung, washed crepe de chine, organza, satin-faced organza, silk chiffon, double-faced satin

Advised by: Clara Henry

Photograph courtesy of Jason Minick

HAILEY DESJARDINS
RHODE ISLAND SCHOOL OF DESIGN

Inspiration: This collection, titled *Grey Jardins*, had several inspirations, including various visual disorders affecting size, depth, and space perception. It was also influenced by the growing and shrinking that Alice undergoes as she enters Wonderland. Together, the designer used these concepts as a springboard to present an idea of something growing and shrinking simultaneously, and what effects that might have on a garment or set of garments. There are representative "large" and "small" elements identifiable in all the pieces, layered over one another to create a sensation of depth. The styling of the looks was loosely inspired by the Beale women of *Grey Gardens*.
Advised by: Catherine Andreozzi
Materials: Felted wool stretch knit, rayon jersey knit, silk/cotton blend knit

Photographs courtesy of Claire Zeller Barclay;
hair & make-up by Sarah Brown

Materials: Sheer wool knit, wool/cotton sheer knit, felted wool stretch knit

Photographs courtesy of Claire Zeller Barclay; hair & make-up by Sarah Brown

Materials: Sheer wool knit, rayon blend knit, felted stretch wool knits, cotton blend jersey knit

Materials: Rayon jersey knit, cotton blend knit, wool blend
fine gauge sweater knit, wool felted stretch knit

*Photographs
courtesy of Claire
Zeller Barclay;
hair & make-up by
Sarah Brown*

Materials: Boiled wool, viscose knit, wool felted stretch
knits, cotton/Lycra blend knit

MEG DEWEY

PHILADELPHIA UNIVERSITY

Inspiration: This collection was inspired by the movie *Factory Girl*, based on the life of Edie Sedgwick. "In the film Edie is portrayed as the life of the party, flirtatious and indulgent; these are the characteristics I wanted my collection to represent."

Materials: Linen, white deerskin

Advised by: Clara Henry

Photograph courtesy of Jason Minick

NEEL EL SHERIF

MOORE COLLEGE OF ART AND DESIGN

Inspiration: This collection of eveningwear garments features timeless ball gowns inspired by the classic femininity of women and female icons of the late 1950s and early '60s.
Materials: Silk, hand-beading
Advised by: Linda Wisner & Le Tran

Photographs courtesy of Paul Loftland

Photograph courtesy of Paul Loftland

REBECCA FORMICHELLA & RITA WATSON

Ring by
Alexis Turner

SAVANNAH COLLEGE OF ART AND DESIGN

Inspiration: The inspiration for this garment is Louise Bourgeois' *Maman* spider sculptures.
Materials: Relief silk, silk lining, chandelier buttons
Advised by: Professors Jason Bunin and Kim Irwin

Photograph courtesy of SCAD

JILLIAN GARVEY

PHILADELPHIA UNIVERSITY

Inspiration: This collection was inspired by the period film *Barry Lyndon* and the novel *Wuthering Heights*. "I wanted to create eveningwear with a romantic, ethereal feeling also giving a sense of femininity and delicacy."

Materials: Mesh netting, silk chiffon, silk taffeta, lace, beads

Advised by: Clara Henry

Photographs courtesy of Jason Minick

TAMARA HALL
WASHINGTON STATE UNIVERSITY

Inspiration: The design was inspired by a police officer's uniform and intended for street wear. Snow pants were deconstructed to make a fitted dress and belts were tied together creating an outer shield. The dress uses belt buckles in a unique way to represent buckling up your seat belt when driving.

Materials: Snow pants, denim skirt, belts, and suede

Advised by: Dr. Yoo Jin Kwon

Photographs courtesy of Robert Hubner

Inspiration: This swimsuit was inspired by the darkness and depth of the ocean. The suit is dark blue, yet shimmers in the sunlight. Embroidered lace was added on the suit to create a unique trim detail. A shine effect was created by having chains on the sides of the bottom of the suit. The suit is strapless and ties in the back so one can get more sun

Materials: 80% nylon with 20% spandex, swimwear tricot, nylon/spandex stretch shoelaces, lace, and metal chains.

Advised by: Dr. Catherine Black

Photographs courtesy of Robert Hubner

Inspiration: Swimwear for lifeguards must provide a balance between visual appeal for wearer, communication of the role of lifeguards as safety personnel, and functional effectiveness during rigorous swimming. One-piece suits are typically uncomfortable and ride up when swimming and bikinis are known to slip or become untied, so a monokini was the best solution. This monokini styling gives the illusion of curves, slims down the body while not being too revealing, yet still has a unique aesthetically pleasing and functional design. The dark color, active pattern, and strong triangle shapes communicates the power this lifeguard has to save lives and maintain order.

Materials: 80% nylon with 20% spandex, swimwear tricot, nylon/spandex stretch shoelaces, and metal buckles.

Advised by: Dr. Carol Salusso

JEFFREY CALDWELL HART

SAVANNAH COLLEGE OF ART AND DESIGN

Inspiration: The inspiration for this garment is the 1938 film depicting the tragic life of Marie Antoinette and the final days of the Ancient Regime, combining Hollywood glamour with a macabre look at Rococo France.

Materials: *Bolero:* double-faced duchess silk; *Corset:* Silk faille, silk, and Lurex chiffon

Advised by: Professors Marie Aja-Herrera and Sachiko Honda

55

Photograph courtesy of SCAD

NICOLE HENDRY
SAVANNAH COLLEGE OF ART AND DESIGN

See page 82, with Megan Lawless

JEN HOBIN
MASSACHUSETTS COLLEGE OF ART AND DESIGN

Inspiration: The history and study of flight is incorporated in men's and women's graphic street wear through handmade silkscreens and painted imagery. Inspirations and subjects include Icarus and Daedalus from Greek mythology, WWII fighter plane nose art, flying machines, old plane diagrams, and Leonardo da Vinci's flight studies. The color palette is drawn from graffiti with a saturated and grimy feel.

Materials: Cotton twill, cotton broadcloth, leather, faux fur, wool jersey, fabric paint

Advised by: Professor Sondra Grace, Chairperson, Fashion Design Department

Photographs courtesy of Richard Bertone

Photographs courtesy of Richard Bertone

Photograph by Essdras M. Suarez/EMS photography, courtesy of Massachusetts College of Art & Design

Materials: Markers, pencils, Adobe Photoshop and Illustrator

STEPHANIE HOFFMANN

ACADEMY OF ART UNIVERSITY, SCHOOL OF FASHION

Inspiration: Surrealism and hand knitting and crochet techniques give this collection the feel of French Couture of the 1920s and '30s. The basis for inspiration was the life of photographer/muse Lee Miller, especially in regards to her connection to surrealist art and artists, and to the photography of Man Ray. The collection is called *Objets d'art* because each piece is a work of art in itself: unique and detailed, pretty and delicate but with a distinct roughness and edge.

Materials: Silk, linen, and modal machine knitting yarn; cotton, silk/linen, silk, and linen hand crochet yarn; 32g black artistic wire; various beads, crystals, and vintage sequins.

Advised by: Simon Ungless, Director of Fashion

Photographs courtesy of Randy Brooke

BRIANNE HOLDEN-BOUSHEY

UNIVERSITY OF WASHINGTON

Inspiration: "My inspiration behind this line was a fabric I found in an old fabric shop. I used this fabric to design a line that has unique features with a feminine look. I used multiple fabrics that added texture to the line, such as velvet and lace. I picked these two fabrics because I wanted the line to be visually pleasing."

Materials: Cotton velvet, lace, hook and eyes, metal zipper

Advised by: Dr. Yoo Jin Kwon and Dr. Catherine Black

Photographs courtesy of Robert Hubner

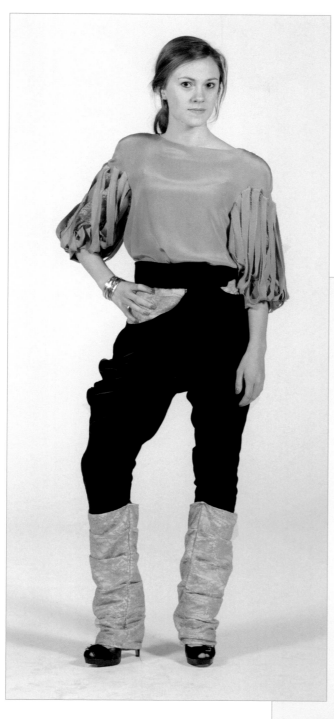

Photographs courtesy of Robert Hubner

Inspiration: "My designs are based on a vintage look with a modern twist. The clothing is for a woman who wants to stand out and is confident with her figure."
Advised by: Dr. Yoo Jin Kwon

Inspiration: "I wanted to design a line that added in a look of tree roots without looking like roots. The look was based on a strong self-expressive woman, someone who shows her personality by what she wears. The line has long lines that lengthen the woman's figure, making her look taller and thinner."
Advised by: Dr. Carol Salusso

Inspiration: The inspiration for this line is the military. The main colors are the military green, and blue. The look balances the masculine lines of the uniforms and the feminine features and curves of the woman.

This line is created for the strong, independent woman who doesn't take "no" for an answer.
Advised by: Dr. Catherine Black

AMANDA HUNT

WASHINGTON STATE UNIVERSITY

Inspiration: The inspiration for this coat comes from a desire to meet both functional *and* aesthetic goals for young women living in colder climates. The coat is fully lined with Thinsulate underneath an exterior of microfiber moleskin, which has a pleasing hand and appearance in addition to being water resistant. The overall silhouette and hand sewn design lines create an elegance that intertwines with and steps above and beyond its functionality. With a zip and a tie, a young woman is off to school or work with class and protection from the elements.

Materials: Microfiber moleskin, Thinsulate, and rayon lining

Advised by: Dr. Carol Salusso

Photograph courtesy of Branden Harvey

Inspiration: This expressive and functional collection of dance garments was designed reflecting the way red jellyfish glorify their Creator by revealing glimpses of His power, joy-filled creativity, and beauty. Each design is composed of multiple pieces with seams emphasizing the organic movement of jellyfish. Each design is intended to respond differently to movement, whether in a fiercely flared skirt, a playfully flipping hem, or in gracefully flowing strips of silk.

Materials: Pencil and watercolors

Advised by: Dr. Yoo Jin Kwon and Dr. Catherine Black

Photographs courtesy of Robert Hubner

Materials: Pencil and watercolors
Advised by: Dr. Yoo Jin Kwon

TIMOTHY K.
PRATT INSTITUTE

Inspiration: "A personally simple process that ends up sounding complex and sadly pretentious when put into words: I approached my designs with more of a fine art perspective, usually being inspired by non-physical cognitive concepts, such as a theory that is intangible or has no actual physical presence. For example these designs are inspired by the concept of human nature told by the likes of Plato, Aristotle, and Freud, as well as the idealistic theories behind Marxism. I create this mental story/mood, and then connect it with a physical creative stimulant, this time being the art of Kazimir Malevich and Franz Kline."

Advised by: Karin Yngvesdotter

Materials: Silk gazar, zibeline, and habotai, and buckram

Photograph courtesy of Vinepod

Photograph courtesy of Shawn Punch

Photograph courtesy of Vinepod

Materials: Silk taffeta, heavy weight taffeta, and netting

Materials: Silk tulle, duchess satin, netting, buckram, and Chantilly lace

Photograph courtesy of Adam Hutchins

Materials: Rice paper, colored pencil

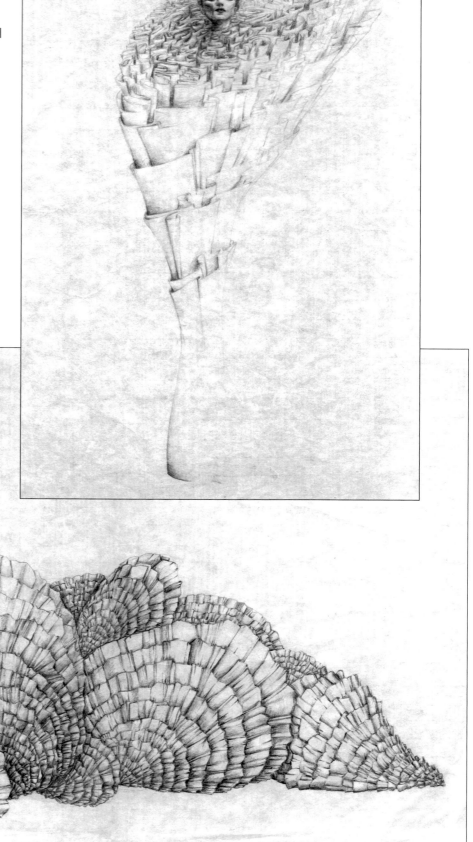

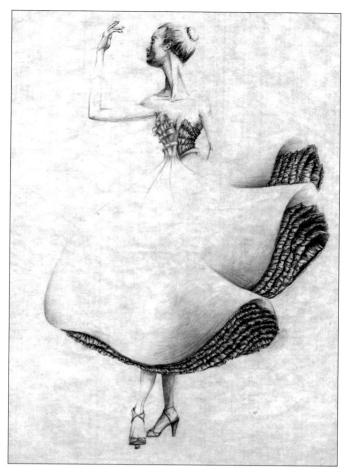

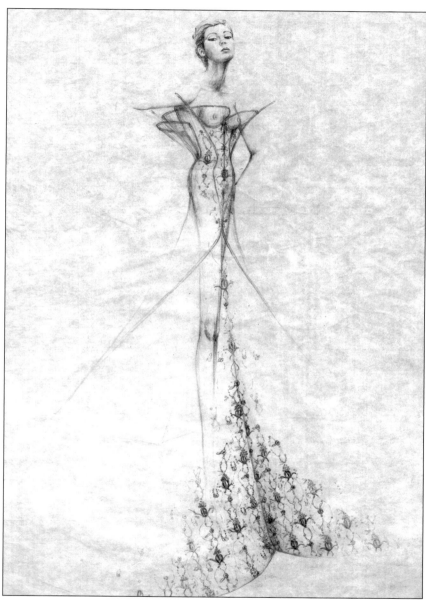

EUNJU KOH

FASHION INSTITUTE OF TECHNOLOGY

Inspiration: "My Fall/Winter collection is inspired by my dream of walking on dusty streets in New York City with a pioneer spirit, exploring a new start with curiosity."

Advised by: Professor Marilyn Hefferen

MODERN NOMADS

YOUNG AE KOO

ACADEMY OF ART UNIVERSITY, SCHOOL OF FASHION

Inspiration: The dark romance of beautiful women is the inspiration for this collection, expressed in dizzying patterns of black and white with the garment structure in feminine form.

Materials: Metallic, wool, and cotton yarns, plastic sequins, and beads.

Advised by: Simon Ungless, Director of Fashion

Photographs courtesy of Randy Brooke

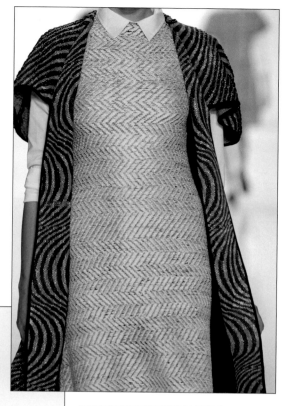

JENNY LAI

RHODE ISLAND SCHOOL OF DESIGN

Inspiration: "My thesis collection, *Intersectellation,* plays with what happens at the intersection of layers of clothing. I wanted to turn dressing into a game of deception where seemingly separate layers of clothing are actually connected in unexpected areas: over the shoulders, through the sleeves, moving fluidly from one body part to another. Most of the collection is made from jute, a 'domestic' fabric commonly used as table covers in Mexico City. I loved its porous and structural quality as well as the saturated, energetic colors…MC Escher's tessellations and Gordon Matta-Clark's dissections of buildings also spoke to me about diverging and converging planes."

Materials: Jute, silk chiffon, machine knit viscose yarn, silk crepe

Advised by: Catherine Andreozzi

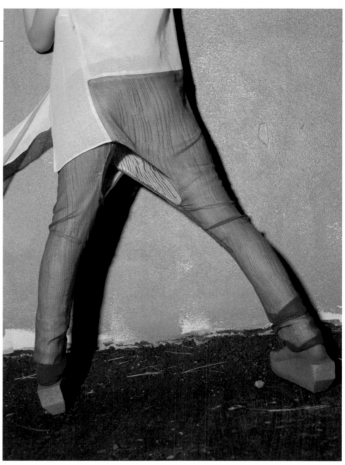

Photographs courtesy of Claire Zeller Barclay; hair & make-up by Sarah Brown

Photographs courtesy of Claire Zeller Barclay; hair & make-up by Sarah Brown

MEGAN LAWLESS   Jewelry by Nicole Hendry

SAVANNAH COLLEGE OF ART AND DESIGN

Inspiration: The inspiration for this look was based on reworking the basic corset and really embracing a woman's figure. "My focus was to utilize the different shapes and style lines to emphasize each curve. I chose a dark palette and masculine fabrics so that each garment would portray the confidence and attitude of the power-house woman that this collection is designed for."

Materials: *Dress:* Silk/wool blend, power mesh; ***Corset:*** Duchess satin

Advised by: Professors Jacqueline Keuler and Anthony S. Miller

Photograph courtesy of SCAD

BRITTANY LEBOLD

MASSACHUSETTS COLLEGE OF ART AND DESIGN

Inspiration: This collection, *Amplify*, features silver metals and subtle textures that glisten under spotlights. Pop colors and vivid prints create a fun energetic punk rock style. Mix and match clothing to rock the streets by day, and the stage by night.

Advised by: Professor Sondra Grace, Chairperson, Fashion Design Department

Photographs courtesy of Ian Dobrowolski

Photograph courtesy of Ian Dobrowolski

Photograph courtesy of Ian Dobrowolski

Photograph Essdras M. Suarez/EMS photography, courtesy of Massachusetts College of Art & Design

YUMI LEE

SAVANNAH COLLEGE OF ART AND DESIGN

Inspiration: The inspiration for this garment is the Victorian era.

Materials: Pleated organza
Advised by: Professors John Bauernfeind & Evelyn Pappas

Photograph courtesy of SCAD

CLAUDIA LIU

RHODE ISLAND SCHOOL OF DESIGN

Inspiration: "For my senior thesis I was inspired by John Isaac, a British sculptor of wax sculptures that are shocking and provoke an emotional response by revealing an 'underlying current of unease and anxiety that identifies our modern way of life and its thinking as somehow warped, disjunctive, and off balance.' As a designer, I enjoy exploring conceptual ideas and translating them into innovative garments."

Materials: Silk jersey, chiffon, tulle, yarn, leather, suede, chains, organza

Advised by: Catherine Andreozzi

Photographs courtesy of Claire Zeller Barclay; hair & make-up by Sarah Brown

CHRISTINA LORD

FASHION INSTITUTE OF TECHNOLOGY

Inspiration: The French bridal trousseaus of the Victorian era—this ensemble harkens back to the days of true craftsmanship in lingerie. This era was a time where couturiers were not simply dressmakers; they were true artisans. With an eye for exquisite and intricate details, the lingerie created were pieces of wearable art.

Materials: Vintage lace, cotton tulle, silk satin ribbon

Advised by: Professor Alexandra Armillas

Photograph courtesy of Doug Congdon-Martin, Schiffer Publishing

Photographs courtesy of Anka Jurena

Inspiration: Inspired by the opulent boudoir elegance the French *"La Belle Époque,"* this ensemble exudes unabashed femininity and sultry romance. This epoch was a time of rich indulgences, luxurious lifestyles, and a bit of debauchery for the highly privileged.

Materials: Metallic brocade, silk satin, silk chiffon, hand beaded Lesage embroidery

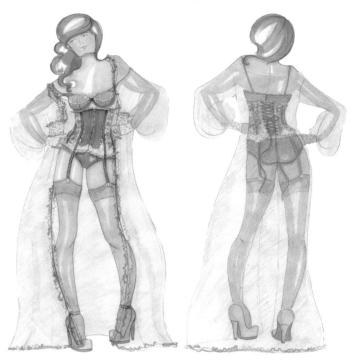

Inspiration: These garments were inspired by the late 1940s film noir, *The Killers*, starring the beautiful femme fatale Ava Gardner. She epitomized the independent, gorgeous woman who has men at her feet. Her classic beauty intertwines with the dark undertones of the '40s film noir genre to make this ensemble something she would wear in the bedroom for some serious seducing.

Materials: Chantilly lace, tulle, satin, mesh

Photographs courtesy of Anka Jurena

Inspiration: Inspired by 1950s sleepwear, this soft and comfortable ensemble emphasizes the supple curves of the feminine form.
Materials: Silk satin, lace, satin ribbon

Inspiration: Inspired by a 1940s Gil Elvgren playful pin-up girl caught in a precarious position in the shower.
Materials: Cotton microfiber, stretch lace

Inspiration: Inspired by the underground nightlife of the 1920s flapper era, where excess and behind-closed-doors freedom were the norm. She is a strong willed, independent woman who plays coy at times, but is an "undercover man-eater."

Advised by: Professor Diane Demers

MARTA MALECK

Rhode Island School of Design

See page 148, collaboration with Scott Stevenson

HALLIE MALITSKY

Drexel University

Inspiration: Using inspiration from the film *My Fair Lady*, the designer created sophisticated cocktail and eveningwear in timeless fabrications. Captured by the elegance and beauty of Audrey Hepburn, she worked to achieve classic, yet modern silhouettes.

Photographs courtesy of Drexel University

JESSICA JUNG MCCORKLE

WASHINGTON STATE UNIVERSITY

Inspiration: "Fly fishing is one of my favorite pastimes. My inspiration for the two-piece dress ensemble came from the first moment the fly lands in the water, breaking the surface and creating the ripple effect. I wanted to incorporate the irregularities of nature and its beauty by using an asymmetrical design in the ripples and one shoulder top. Colors found in the two-piece ensemble are colors of early morning—the best time to fly fish. When the sun rises, it casts its bright yellow light on the dark river water and reflects a brilliant glow on the surface of the water."

Materials: 100% cotton sateen, using low impact, fiber reactive dye to achieve colors, 100% silk lining, silver chain, and real fly fishing flies

Advised by: Dr. Yoo Jin Kwon and Dr. Catherine Black

Photographs courtesy of Robert Hubner

Inspiration: The inspiration from the dress came from the growing global trend of sustainability and the slogan "Reuse, Recycle, Reduce," by reinventing a piece of classic art by Monet and making it a true piece of wearable art. Monet, considered a groundbreaking artist of his time, is most famous for impressionist paintings like *Poppy Field near Argenteuil*.
Materials: Canvas
Advised by: Dr. Yoo Jin Kwon

BETHANY MEULENERS

ACADEMY OF ART UNIVERSITY, SCHOOL OF FASHION

Inspiration: A girl playing "dress up" before going out, grabbing several different layers and throwing them on, letting them land where they land. Visual inspiration was derived from 3D images without the use of the 3D glasses, futuristic photo images, and Duchamp's *Nude Descending a Staircase*. All of these have one thing in common: The visual effect of more than one image (sometimes the same image several times) layered on top of the other but slightly off kilter. This translated into the combination of knits and wovens, making them into the different layers but still as part of the same fabric or garment.

Materials: Recycled surplus military blanket for the jackets, as well as mohair, wool, and metallic yarns, silk chiffon.

Advised by: Simon Ungless, Director of Fashion

Photographs courtesy of Randy Brooke

JULIE MOLLO
PRATT INSTITUTE

Inspiration: "I believe that one should be excited to get dressed every morning, and feel like they are off to a party when they may only be running some errands. Inspired by shapes, love, the 1950s, the city of New York, and anything that sparkles, my clothes are youthful but sophisticated, urban but classy, quirky, witty, and above all fun."

Materials: Acid washed denim, gold metal zipper, tulle, satin, and jersey

Photographs courtesy of Katrina Eugenia

Materials: Stretch cotton, tulle, cotton, gingham ruffles, and white and sequined ric rac

Materials: Acid washed denim, tulle, metallic taffeta, printed cotton, metal zippers

CHOLLY MOLTHAN

WWW.CHOLLYMOLTHAN.COM

MASSACHUSETTS COLLEGE OF ART AND DESIGN

Inspiration: In this collection, *Natural Selection*, a free-wheeling attitude embraces early depictions of natural history for their folk art charm.

Advised by: Professor Sondra Grace, Chairperson, Fashion Design Department

Photographs courtesy of Richard Bertone

YOKO OKUDA

FASHION INSTITUTE OF TECHNOLOGY

Inspiration: Very much inspired by the dark tone and storyline of the *Grimm's Fairy Tales*, these clothes tell a story of a beautiful girl who wandered off into the forest and is now forever lost. She has no desire to return home and continues her search for somewhere to go.

Materials: Variety of four cottons, lace trims, black dye, bleach, Bokuju (Japanese calligraphy ink)

Advised by: Marlene Middlemiss

Photographs courtesy of John Zinonos

Photographs courtesy of John Zinonos

Inspiration: These designs, for an active lifestyle, combine the grunge look of bandages and swirling effects of the wind. Each piece is very versatile and retains an edgy look for the young and active skater who is always on the go.
Materials: Markers, pencil, colored pencil
Advised by: Anna Kipper

BRITTANY OLIVER

FASHION INSTITUTE OF TECHNOLOGY

Inspiration: "My inspiration is derived from a customer
   I can relate to. Chic, flirtatious femininity."
Materials: Wool, chiffon

Photographs courtesy of Jani Zubkovs

Photographs courtesy of Jani Zubkovs

Inspiration: "When I illustrate I am aiming to create an extension of a perpetual mood…Soft, subtle, fluid, feminine."
Materials: Marker, pencil

RIONA FAITH O'MALLEY

DREXEL UNIVERSITY

Inspiration: This senior collection was inspired by the "armor" of various types of arthropods such as spiders, scorpions, insects, and crabs. The designer used cuir bouilli, a medieval technique for shaping and hardening leather, to create exaggerated armor-like forms emphasizing certain areas of the body.
Materials: Leather

Photographs courtesy of Drexel University

STEVEN OO

Inspiration: The clean lines in the work of Italian architect Massimiliano Fuksas. "The clean lines and graceful curves were translated into garments as I draped each of my designs. In my collection, there are three different design elements that I have employed to tie all the pieces together. The long draped curves are used around the shoulder, on the back, and on the side to create dramatic silhouettes. Each of the knit stitches has extreme textures that are balanced by the traditional rib stitch, which is recurring in each garment in a variety of ways. Lastly, cutout details from the architecture of Fuksas are used in the garments to expose the garments worn underneath as well as the accessories."

Materials: Super merino wool, chunky merino wool, cotton pique.

Advised by: Simon Ungless, Director of Fashion

Photographs courtesy of Randy Brooke

Photographs courtesy of Randy Brooke

ASHLEY PAHLER

Inspiration: The theme for this collection is "vintage carnival." Soft fabrics reflect femininity and whimsy while the structure introduces the quirky shapes of Ferris wheels and carousels. Each look features a playful concept like hand beading, embroidery, and hand sewing.

Photographs courtesy of Drexel University

MAKEN IMCHA PAYNE
SAVANNAH COLLEGE OF ART AND DESIGN

Inspiration: This garment was inspired by architecture, specifically the dynamic towers in Dubai.

Materials: Ottoman fabric, chiffon, taffeta, printed Indian raw silk

Advised by: Professors Jason Bunin and Kim Irwin

Photograph courtesy of SCAD

LINDSAY PERKINS
RHODE ISLAND SCHOOL OF DESIGN

Inspiration: "My thesis collection, *Frail*, was initially inspired by my research into Japanese clothing and Samurai armor. As a result I started thinking about the nature of armor and vulnerability, not only in the context of clothing, but even vulnerabilities and frailties in my own life. My goal was to express these self-reflections through loose fitting, simple shapes, and natural colors. As I was draping on the form I used sheers and layers, handmade ceramic accessories, and open spaces on the body to communicate these ideas."

Advised by: Catherine Andreozzi

Materials: Fully fashioned machine knit top with porcelain detail; linen shorts

Photographs courtesy of Ricky Chapman

Photographs courtesy of Ricky Chapman

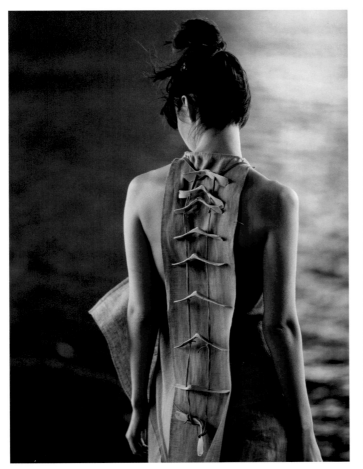

Materials: Machine knit top with woven panel; layered
linen pants; terra cotta and leather accessory

Materials: Draped linen top with terra cotta details; linen shorts

Photographs courtesy of Ricky Chapman

Materials: Silk and sheer cotton top with heavy linen pants; silk, porcelain, and leather jewelry piece

EMILY POLLARD

Savannah College of Art and Design

Inspiration: This garment was inspired by ice/encasement.

Materials: Silk satin organza

Advised by: Professors Christopher McDonnell and Evelyn Pappas

Photograph courtesy of SCAD

MARINA POPSKA

ACADEMY OF ART UNIVERSITY, SCHOOL OF FASHION

Inspiration: This collection is inspired by nature, humanity, and the 'chaos' of color and texture; the idea that human and tree could become one creature.

Materials: Merino wool and bamboo yarns, nylon power mesh for support pieces

Advised by: Simon Ungless, Director of Fashion

Photographs courtesy of Randy Brooke

Photographs courtesy of Randy Brooke

Photographs courtesy of Randy Brooke

ERIKA RAE

Inspiration: The inspiration for these garments was The Day of the Dead. "I am inspired by the world… fusing traditions, mixing cultures, and celebrating one another."

Materials: Dress – embroidered cotton, fabric flowers, and miniature plastic toys and bones, hand embroidered with yarn hem.

Vest outfit – embroidered 100% silk, printed cottons, tulle; recycled burlap, yarn, and felt vest with hand painted cotton lining, knit top, and leggings

Advised by: FIT faculty

Photograph courtesy of Doug Congdon-Martin, Schiffer Publishing

Inspiration: These illustrations are a fusion of Eastern and Western styles and traditions.

Materials: Watercolor paint, colored pencils, markers, crayons, and make-up
Advised by: FIT faculty

DELPHINA STAR RODRIGUEZ

ACADEMY OF ART UNIVERSITY, SCHOOL OF FASHION

See page 30, collaboration with Yuzuan Cheng

JESSICA HELEN SAIDIAN

SAVANNAH COLLEGE OF ART AND DESIGN

Inspiration: The inspiration for this garment was to create a unique costume for *A Clockwork Orange* that combines feminine Victorian silhouettes with masculine structural shapes.

Materials: Double-faced upholstery fabric of a cotton/rayon blend

Advised by: Professors Sachiko Honda and Jason Paul McCarthy

Photograph courtesy of SCAD

ASHLEY B. SCOTT

MOORE COLLEGE OF ART AND DESIGN

Inspiration: *Neon-Guard* is an eclectic sportswear collection that fuses traditional British military uniform and Japanese street fashion. The designer was especially moved by the uniforms of past generations and their remarkable stories that allow a glimpse into the past.

Materials: Leather, Lycra, neon waterproof polyester

Advised by: Linda Wisner & Le Tran

Photographs courtesy of Paul Loftland

DOMINIQUE SCOTT
MASSACHUSETTS COLLEGE OF ART AND DESIGN

Inspiration: *Corvus Columba* is a lingerie line inspired by the transition from chaos to tranquility through birds: the mourning dove and raven.
Materials: Organza, feathers
Advised by: Professor Sondra Grace, Chairperson, Fashion Design Department

Photographs courtesy of Stephen Cicco

Photograph courtesy of Ian Dobrowolski

YEE MAN SO
Rings by Kathleen A. Staton, Shop SCAD & Virginia Wynne, Shop SCAD

SAVANNAH COLLEGE OF ART AND DESIGN

Inspiration: The inspiration for this garment is bridal flowers.

Materials: Organza

Advised by: Professors Marie Aja-Herrera and Evelyn Pappas

Photograph courtesy of SCAD

MARINA SOLOMATNIKOVA

ACADEMY OF ART UNIVERSITY, SCHOOL OF FASHION

Inspiration: Georgia O'Keefe's paintings, which show pieces in nature from an unusual perspective—images of flowers on the horse skull against a sandy surface; mother of pearl with colors changing from pure white to night black; white seashells contrasting against the multicolored dark background—all of these elements found their way into the collection. The combination of tough natural forms with fragile, airy elements is seen in the marriage of chiffon and suede. The pulsating rhythms of O'Keefe's multilayered landscapes inspired pleats and trapunto designs. Curvy, continuous, flowing lines in her paintings gave birth to complex drapes and silhouettes in the garments.

Materials: Suede and silk organza

Advised by: Simon Ungless, Director of Fashion

Photograph courtesy of Randy Brooke

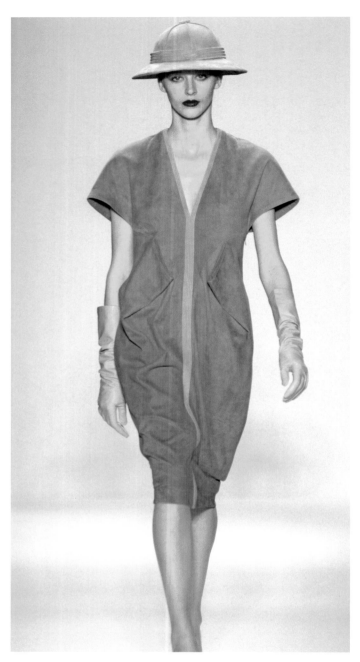

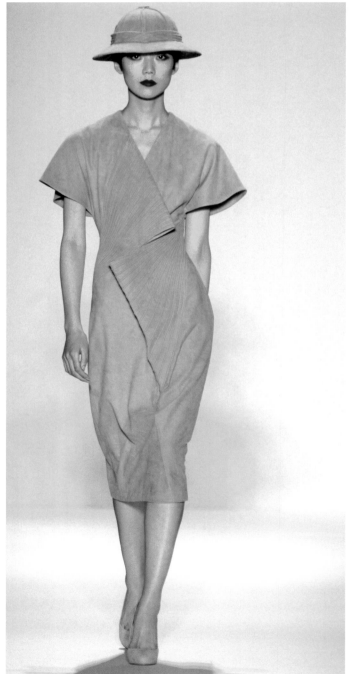

Photographs courtesy of Randy Brooke

LAUREN STARK

Inspiration: "My collection is a military-inspired line that is a mash up of long velvet coats, short jersey jackets, skinny wool pants, and detailed shirts. It is designed around guys who are about to graduate college or have started to make the transition into their new career. These men are independent, and are very style conscious."

Materials: Velvet, jersey, stretch wool, cotton shirting

Advised by: Jongeun Rhee, Ph.D.

Photograph courtesy of Andrew Olson

Photographs courtesy of Andrew Olson

KATHLEEN A. STATON

SAVANNAH COLLEGE OF ART AND DESIGN

See page 142, with Yee Man So

SCOTT STEVENSON Marta Maleck, textile design

RHODE ISLAND SCHOOL OF DESIGN

Inspiration: This design collaboration, *Horse Eating Sundance*, was inspired by the ephemeral existence of once-mighty civilizations, primarily referencing ancient Greek and Aztec civilizations. The design of the clothing references the shape of the Möbius strip, while also relating to primitive yet sophisticated pattern designs, and portraying the cyclical patterns of our societies. The weaving techniques, devoré, and jacquard designs used in certain garments reinvent early fabric construction techniques, while examining topographical views and weathering effects of each culture's respective ruins. These anthropological ideas were then juxtaposed with the attitude of reggae artist Chaka Demus and designer Paul Poiret.

Advised by: Catherine Andreozzi

Materials: *Top:* hand-dyed silk georgette, hand-dyed silk/linen blend, and tulle; *Pants:* multi-fiber jacquard, pony hide, and linen

Photographs courtesy of Kirsten McNally

Materials: *Vest:* multi-fiber jacquard; *Top:* hand-dyed silk/Lycra blend crepe; *Skirt:* hand-dyed, power washed silk/Lycra blend crepe

Photographs courtesy of Kirsten McNally

Materials: *Coat:* hand-dyed silk organza, hand-dyed silk/linen blend with devoré details on pockets, embroidered with ostrich feathers and needle- punched with silk noil; *Dress:* hand-dyed silk/linen with hand-woven, hand painted appliqués,

KERRY ANN STOKES

MASSACHUSETTS COLLEGE OF ART AND DESIGN

Inspiration: In this collection, *Electric Metamorphosis*, wearable sculptures that emulate insects emerge from fabric manipulations. Textures come from beetle shells, moth fur, and scaled praying mantises. Shapes reference butterfly wings and colors from all of the brilliantly painted insects that decorate our world.

Advised by: Professor Sondra Grace, Chairperson, Fashion Design Department

Photographs courtesy of Clark Graham

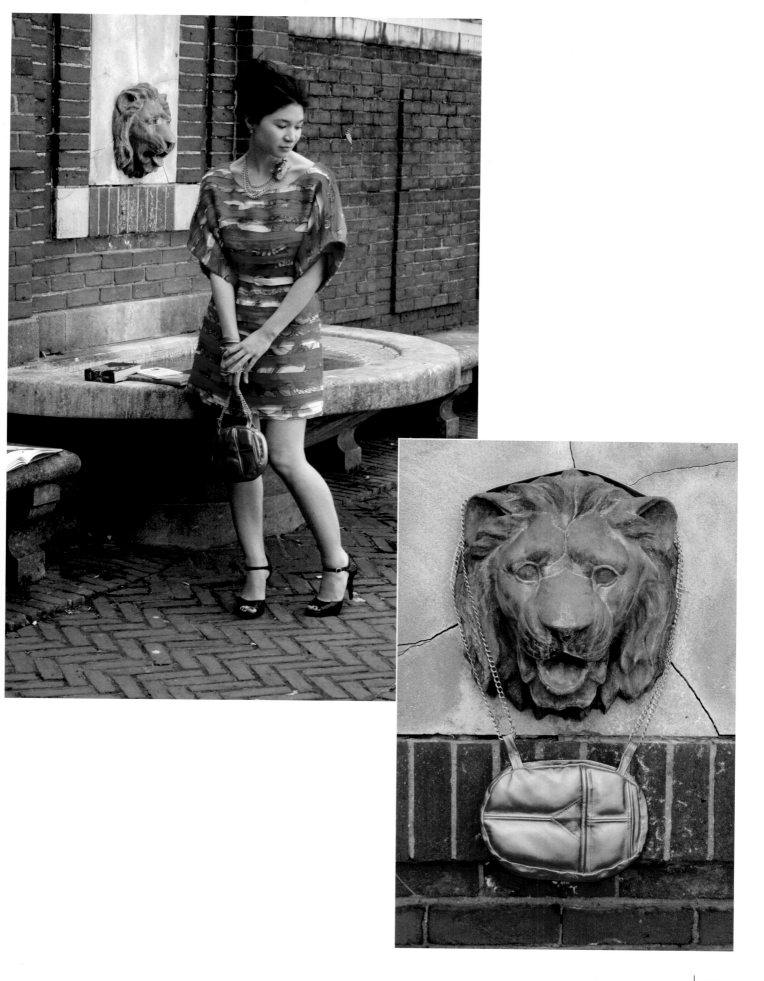

Photograph courtesy of Essdras M. Suarez/EMS Photography, courtesy of Massachusetts College of Art & Design

DOM STREATER

MOORE COLLEGE OF ART AND DESIGN

Inspiration: *Pivotal Chic*, my senior collection, was inspired by the growing cycling community around the world. I decided to design garments that serve the dual purpose of being functional and stylish. For example, the clear raincoats allow bikers clothing to remain dry yet still express their personal style.

Materials: Jersey, denim, satin, felt, clear vinyl

Advised by: Linda Wisner & Le Tran

Photograph courtesy of Jeff Cohn/FashionandAdvertising.com

Photographs courtesy of Paul Loftland

KIMBERLY L. STROMBERG

MOORE COLLEGE OF ART AND DESIGN

Inspiration: This classic, woodsman-inspired collection features timeless separates designed for the all-American male. *Cabin Fever* offers men from ages 18 to 44 a forever-stylish blend of comfort and tradition.

Materials: Silk cottons, rib knits, hand embroideries

Advised by: Linda Wisner & Cheryl Washington

Photographs courtesy of Jeff Cohn/FashionandAdvertising.com

CHRISTINE MY LINH TONG

MOORE COLLEGE OF ART AND DESIGN

Inspiration: This design was inspired by Roman and various historical war headdresses. It focuses on the beauty of war costume.

Materials: Paper, clay, copper wire, fabric, and spray paint

Advised by: Linda Wisner & Le Tran

Photographs courtesy of Victor/Studio 206

Inspiration: This collection was inspired by vintage Victorian dolls.
Materials: Cotton and polyester blend
Advised by: Linda Wisner & Le Tran

*Photographs courtesy of Victor/**Studio 206***

Photographs courtesy of Victor/Studio 206

ALEXIS TURNER

SAVANNAH COLLEGE OF ART AND DESIGN

See page 47, with Rebecca Formichella & Rita Wilson

THE TWENTYTEN
the twentyten are Nina Zilka, David J. Krause, & Jeff Dodd

PRATT INSTITUTE

Inspiration: For this collection the twentyten started with the British occupation of India and the idea of military influences more drapey, less constructed pieces. The collection grew into the idea of tactile fabrications, and garments that felt like they had been touched and worked with before the wearer owned them. The designers created kinetic, textural pieces that utilized yarn, faux fur, and hair, and played with draping and structural elements in the same garment, looking to contrast the everyday with the unexpected.

Advised by: Robin Mollicone

Materials: Peach skin microfiber and acrylic yarn

Photographs courtesy of Evan Browning

Materials: Cotton twill, polyester faux fur, cotton French terry, gunmetal rivets

Materials: Cotton French terry and polyester faux fur

Materials: Cotton twill, gun metal rivets, and polyester faux fur

Materials: Hand painted cotton French terry and black French terry

Materials: Cotton twill and cotton French terry, peach skin microfiber

Photographs courtesy of Evan Browning

Materials: Acrylic yarn and cotton French terry

Materials: Cotton French terry and hand painted cotton shirting

Materials: Cotton twill, cotton French terry, cotton shirting

SAMIRA VARGAS

MASSACHUSETTS COLLEGE OF ART AND DESIGN

Inspiration: A collection inspired by musical instruments that create the rhythm that captivates one's senses; *Merengue* features sculptural silhouettes in animal skins creating a mixture of different textures and fabrics to connect with the music within.

Advised by: Professor Sondra Grace, Chairperson, Fashion Design Department

Photograph courtesy of Richard Bertone

Photograph by Essdras M. Suarez/EMS photography, courtesy of Massachusetts College of Art & Design

AMANDA VEREB

PHILADELPHIA UNIVERSITY

Inspiration: This collection was inspired by plastic surgery, and the FX television show "Nip/Tuck" in particular. "I was inspired by the whole idea of identity; the ideal of being perfect, feminizing or masculinizing yourself...Linear aspects on each garment represent the straight cut lines a surgeon has to make in order to create flawless and perfect recovery...The clothing patterns and garments have symmetry with artificial asymmetric lines, fake wraps, and closures that give the audience an idea of artificial perfection. Monochromatic colors give a clean and sterile look, while pops of red represent incisions made by a scalpel. Outerwear signifies bandages for recovery and the graphic tees show the real face of plastic surgery."

Materials: Jersey, spandex, wool, cotton woven, cotton/spandex blend, satin flannel, zippers, screen print

Advised by: Clara Henry

Photograph courtesy of Jason Minick

HANNAH J. WALKER

UNIVERSITY OF WISCONSIN-STOUT

Inspiration: "Love, family, and tradition have inspired me to create *Josephine*, a collection of comfort-based yet elegant bridal gowns. For centuries a wedding dress has symbolized the union and love between two people."

Materials: Silk, jersey
Advised by: Dr. Gindy Neidermyer

Photograph courtesy of Alisha Bube

Photographs courtesy of Alisha Bube

RITA WATSON

SAVANNAH COLLEGE OF ART AND DESIGN

See page 47, collaboration with Rebecca Formichella

JENN WEBB

WWW.COROFLOT.COM/JENNNICOLEWEBB

MASSACHUSETTS COLLEGE OF ART AND DESIGN

Inspiration: In this collection, *Re+Generated*, on a post-apocalyptic earth survivors rise out of the ashes of decay. Rusted colors mirror depleted landscapes and decrepit buildings. Corroded metal and plastic remnants from an over-industrialized past are molded into armor. Deterioration can bring forth regeneration.

Advised by: Professor Sondra Grace, Chairperson, Fashion Design Department

Photographs by Essdras M. Suarez/EMS photography, courtesy of Massachusetts College of Art & Design

Photographs courtesy of Patrick Brassard

RACHEL WENDLING

PHILADELPHIA UNIVERSITY

Inspiration: The inspiration for this collection lies behind the wrought iron gates of Charles Dickens' novel *Great Expectations*. The collection is a modern interpretation of the imagery found in the novel, and appeals to the sensibilities of the Victorian era. Detailed accents and couture sewing techniques are a subtle allusion to the novel's themes of innocence and the delicate femininity of true beauty.

Advised by: Clara Henry

Materials: Hand-beaded wire mesh, feathers, duchess silk satin, silk chiffon, silk charmeuse, silk ombre, and organza

Photographs courtesy of Jason Minick

Inspiration: This collection, called *Rain or Shine*, was inspired by the construction of sailboats and the movement of the wind.

Materials: Duchess satin, charmeuse, chiffon, and a raw silk "boat rope"

MEGAN ANNE WENDT

UNIVERSITY OF WISCONSIN-STOUT

Inspiration: The concept of this collection, *The Age of the Game*, came from the antiquity of vintage sports equipment. For decades, the rules, theory, and age of Olympic sports have evolved. *The Age of the Game* focuses on transformation, or evolution of clothing. Each hood utilizes various fastener systems to allow transformation into an original hood style, collar or scarf. Flatlock stitch detailing replicates the stitches in a baseball, lacrosse stick or football while the overall feeling evokes a historic appeal with an innovative twist.

Materials: Double knit, Tencel, French terry, wool knit, corduroy

Advised by: Dr. Gindy Neidermyer

Photographs courtesy of Eric Hampton

Photographs courtesy of Eric Hampton

VIRGINIA WYNNE

SAVANNAH COLLEGE OF ART AND DESIGN

See page 142, with Ye Man So

DAVID YOO

RHODE ISLAND SCHOOL OF DESIGN

Inspiration: Inspired by photography of the 1890s and the stories told through each picture, the black and white imagery of the photographs leaves much to the viewers' interpretation. The lack of color was a way to focus on the use of different textures, fabrics, and silhouettes. The backbone of the collection is tailoring and the ability to fit the body of both men and women without the typical constraints of "men's wear" or "women's wear."

Materials: Wool, tulle, cotton, neoprene, silk, jersey
Advised by: Catherine Andreozzi

Photographs courtesy of Andre Herrero

Photographs courtesy of Andre Herrero

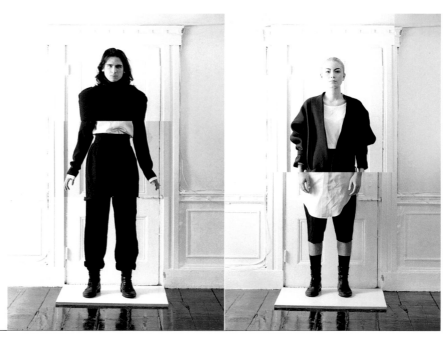

THE
DESIGNERS
BY SCHOOL

ACADEMY OF ART UNIVERSITY, SCHOOL OF FASHION

DREXEL UNIVERSITY

FASHION INSTITUTE OF TECHNOLOGY

MASSACHUSETTS COLLEGE OF ART AND DESIGN

Vargas, Samira
174

Hobin, Jen
53

Webb, Jenn
182

LeBold, Brittany
83

MOORE COLLEGE OF ART AND DESIGN

Molthan, Cholly
104

Boston, Leah C.
18

Scott, Dominique
140

El Sherif, Neel
45

Stokes, Kerry Ann
152

Scott, Ashley B.
139

SAVANNAH COLLEGE OF ART & DESIGN

UNIVERSITY OF MINNESOTA

UNIVERSITY OF WISCONSIN-STOUT

WASHINGTON STATE UNIVERSITY